THE BEST JOB EVER

Author

Ian F. Mahaney

PowerKiDS press.

New York

Published in 2015 by The Rosen Publishing Group, Inc.
29 East 21st Street, New York, NY 10010

First Edition

Editor: Caitie McAneney
Book Design: Katelyn Heinle

Library of Congress Cataloging-in-Publication Data

Mahaney, Ian F.
Author / by Ian F. Mahaney.
p. cm. — (The best job ever)
Includes index.
ISBN 978-1-4994-0113-4 (pbk.)
ISBN 978-1-4994-0087-8 (6-pack)
ISBN 978-1-4994-0106-6 (library binding)
1. Authorship — Vocational guidance — Juvenile literature. I. Mahaney, Ian F. II. Title.
PN153.M35 2015
808—d23

Manufactured in the United States of America

CPSIA Compliance Information: Batch #CW15PK: For Further Information contact Rosen Publishing, New York, New York at 1-800-237-9932

Contents

A CAREER AS AN AUTHOR

Think about the best book you've ever read. Maybe you loved that book because of the characters or the **plot**. Maybe you couldn't put the book down! That book was written by an author. An author is someone who writes for a living. If you love reading and writing, a **career** as an author might be perfect for you!

Some authors write fiction, or stories that aren't real. Others write nonfiction, which is based on real facts or events. Some authors write for children and young adults, while others write for adults. Some authors write magazine or newspaper articles, while others write songs or poetry.

Anything you read was once written by an author—even the writing on your cereal box!

AUTHOR BENEFITS

Publishing companies pay authors for the right to publish their work. The author gets a share of the money the book makes in sales.

Authors get to explore and write about their favorite subjects. Some authors love to **research** and write about science or history. Other authors love to use their imagination to create characters.

Authors are able to reach out to their readers through their writing. They try to make their writing **relatable** and interesting. Once authors grab their readers' attention, they can teach readers something new. Authors can also help readers feel better about something they're going through.

Judy Blume wrote many novels for children and young adults, including *Blubber* and *Freckle Juice*. Many readers like her books because they're very relatable.

Judy Blume

LEARNING TO WRITE

Most people learn the basics of writing in elementary school. You could probably write a story right now! To improve writing skills, **aspiring** authors sometimes take special creative writing classes in high school. Some authors study writing in college.

College teachers, or professors, teach writing students how to read deeply, research, and write reports and stories. Many fiction authors study English in college. They read books that are classics, or well-known for being great. They also learn how to write about books.

Many nonfiction authors study another subject, such as science or history. They learn all about that subject before writing about it.

AUTHOR BIO: JEFF KINNEY

Jeff Kinney is a children's author who writes the *Diary of a Wimpy Kid* series. He studied at the University of Maryland, where he wrote a comic strip for his college newspaper.

Some authors go to school after they finish college to learn creative writing. Other authors believe that writing can be learned and practiced without a college degree.

READING AND WRITING

Authors gain career skills by reading and writing. Reading books gives authors examples of great writing. It can help authors think up a new story or learn about new subjects. Reading helps authors think of new ways of writing about their ideas.

To become good writers, authors write as often as they can. They can practice writing stories for themselves or turn them in to writing contests. Aspiring authors can also write for their school newspaper. This is often an author's first time working with an editor. Editors help authors fix mistakes and make necessary changes to polish the author's work.

You can start practicing to be an author right now. Go to your local library and check out books that interest you. Just keep reading!

LANDING A JOB

Authors find jobs writing books, magazine articles, **blogs**, and newspaper stories. Some writers work for movies, television, or radio. Many writers also earn their living as copywriters. Copywriters write for advertising companies to help sell a product. To land these jobs, writers usually have to show a company a sample of their writing. Aspiring authors put together a portfolio, which is a collection of their best writing samples.

Some writers and authors find jobs writing for a certain company, but many are freelancers. Freelancers are independent writers who do work for different companies.

AUTHOR BIO: DAN GREENBURG

Dan Greenburg writes for both adults and children. He began his career as a copywriter and went on to be a published author. He's the author of the *Maximum Boy* and *The Zack Files* series.

Some authors write books and then sell them to a publishing company. This is an example of freelance work.

THE WRITING LIFE

What do authors do every day? Many authors don't have to go to an office building or follow a regular **schedule**. Instead, their schedules are often **flexible**, and many can write from home. Many authors make their own plans and decide when and where to work. Some authors write well in the morning, while others work better in the afternoon or at night.

Many authors like to write in coffee shops. J.K. Rowling wrote the *Harry Potter* series from a coffee shop called the Elephant House in Edinburgh, Scotland.

Many authors need a silent place to work, so they stay home. Others work better in public places like coffee shops or libraries. All authors have one thing in common, though—they spend their work time writing.

WRITING A BOOK

Most authors write a certain kind of book, or genre (ZHAHN-ruh). Genres include adult fiction, children's fiction, poetry, nonfiction, and **fantasy**. Shel Silverstein was an author who wrote books of children's poems. Doris Kearns Goodwin writes history books for adults. Whether writing for children or adults, authors have to understand their readers and use language the readers will understand.

When an author writes in multiple genres, they often use a pen name. A pen name is a name an author uses to hide their real name. One of the most famous pen names is Dr. Seuss. His real name was Theodor Seuss Geisel.

Do you like fiction or nonfiction better? Some people like fiction because it tells a story, while others like nonfiction because it gives facts.

AUTHOR BIO: CHRISTOPHER PAOLINI

Christopher Paolini is a children's fantasy author. He became a best-selling author with his first book, *Eragon*, when he was only 19 years old.

Most authors hope to be published one day. Some authors self-publish, which is when they either post their work online or pay to have books printed. Most authors send their writing to publishing companies. Publishing companies can decide to buy the book so they can sell it.

AUTHOR BIO: SUZANNE COLLINS

Suzanne Collins is an American author who is best known for writing *The Hunger Games* series. She also wrote the best-selling *Underland Chronicles* series and wrote for several children's television shows.

Once a company buys an author's book, the author works with an editor to make the book great. The book is edited many times before it's printed and ready to sell!

Before an author sells a book, they need to find an agent. Agents help authors find and work with editors at publishing companies. Finding an agent can be hard, but an author can increase their chances by sending their best work to many agents. It also helps to network, or make connections with people in the publishing world.

JOBS RELATED TO WRITING

There are many jobs related to writing and publishing. **Designers** plan how books and magazines will look. Illustrators draw pictures for books, especially children's books. Editors work for publishing companies, magazines, and newspapers. Publishers hire marketing and sales staff to sell their books.

There are many other writing jobs, too. Screenwriters write movies and television shows. Playwrights write plays to be performed on stage. Computer and medical businesses hire writers that can make **complicated** ideas easy to understand for customers. These are often called technical writers. Book reviewers for magazines and newspapers write about books they've read.

> If you like writing and editing, you might want to be an editor. If you like writing and science, you might want to be a technical writer. There are many jobs in writing!

A STORY TO TELL

Being an author is hard work. An author may have to work long hours to meet deadlines. Deadlines are set times when a piece of writing has to be finished. Sometimes authors have trouble finding the right words to write. That's called having writer's block.

Despite the hard work, writing is a great career, especially for a creative person. Authors get to write about things that interest them. They often make their own schedule and choose their own projects. Their words are shared with hundreds, thousands, or even millions of people! Authors have a story to tell. Do you?

Glossary

aspiring: Strongly wanting to achieve a goal.

blog: A personal website on which someone writes about their thoughts and opinions.

career: A job.

complicated: Hard to understand.

designer: Someone who makes plans for how something will look.

fantasy: A genre with settings and characters that often have magical powers or other unrealistic features.

flexible: Able to change.

plot: The events that happen in a story.

publishing: Having to do with producing a written work and presenting it to the public.

relatable: Something people can connect with.

research: To study something carefully to find out more about it.

schedule: A plan of what one has to do at certain times.

Index

Websites

Due to the changing nature of Internet links, PowerKids Press has developed an online list of websites related to the subject of this book. This site is updated regularly. Please use this link to access the list: www.powerkidslinks.com/bje/auth